Coloring book for adults and kids amazing dove image for design

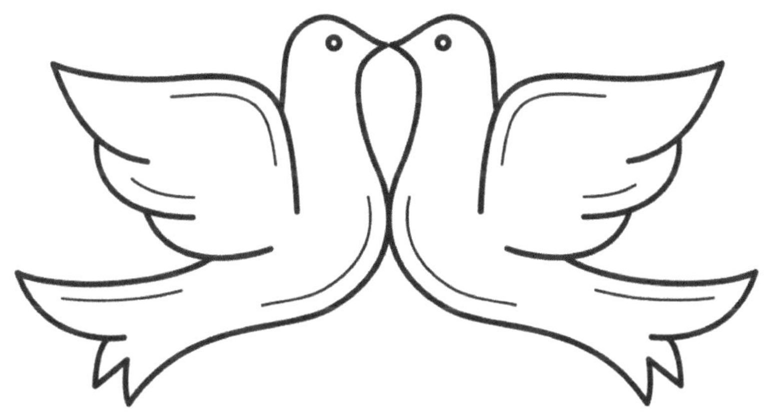

This coloring book is belongs to

____

____

____

Pigeons
Set

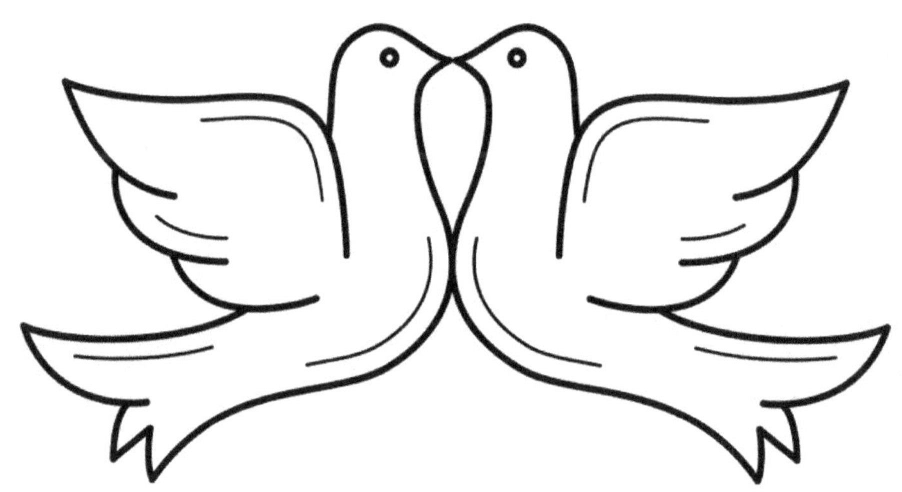

www.ingramcontent.com/pod-product-compliance
Lightning Source LLC
Chambersburg PA
CBHW081244250726
48654CB00012B/1469